MATTHEW
Prophecy Fulfilled

ELIZABETH VIERA TALBOT

Pacific Press® Publishing Association
Nampa, Idaho
Oshawa, Ontario, Canada
www.pacificpress.com

Cover design by Gerald Lee Monks
Cover design resources from John Steel
Inside design by Aaron Troia

Additional copies of this book are available by calling toll-free
1-800-765-6955 or by visiting http://www.AdventistBookCenter
.com.

ISBN 13: 978-0-8163-2353-1
ISBN 10: 0-8163-2353-4

10 11 12 13 14 • 6 5 4 3 2

Dedication

I dedicate this booklet
to my husband, Patrick,
my parents, Juan Carlos and Alicia,
and to Jesus, my Kinsman-Redeemer.

Acknowledgments

I want to thank some very important people in my life. First, I want to thank my husband, Patrick, for his love for the gospel of Jesus Christ and his passion to preach it. He is my gospel soul mate, and I will be forever grateful to God for bringing Patrick into my life. Next, I want to thank my parents, Dr. Juan Carlos and Alicia Viera, for instilling the love of Jesus in me from my early childhood, as they devoted their entire lives to the preaching of the gospel as well. Incidentally, I used to preach to my dolls when I was only three years old. I thank heaven for the blessing of godly parents. I want to thank all my friends and colleagues who helped me revise this manuscript: Shirley Adams; my husband, Patrick; my dad, Dr. J. C. Viera; and Dr. Alfonso Valenzuela. I want to particularly highlight the contribution made by my close friend Dr. Aivars Ozolins, who spent many hours editing these words.

I will be forever indebted to my professor and mentor, Dr. Lynn Losie. He was the first to introduce me to a serious scholarly study of the Gospels, and his class, The Gospel's Witness to Christ, forever changed my life and my ministry. Many of the insights you will find in this booklet have come from him and are used with his permission. I know that his contribution in my ministerial life was providential. For several years now, I have been given the opportunity to teach the same class myself, and I pray that God may impact my students the way he impacted me through Dr. Losie.

I also want to thank the Voice of Prophecy and my daily broadcast cohost, Mike Tucker, who encouraged me to write this booklet. It is such a privilege for me to work with Mike. His love for the gospel inspires me. This is the happiest time in my professional life, and I am so thankful for the opportunities to preach and teach the gospel every day. I also want to thank the Pacific Press® team for embarking with the Voice of Prophecy on this venture. Thank you for your willingness to print this booklet in such a short time. Thank you!

Contents

Introduction

Many years ago, I became fascinated with the four Gospels: Matthew, Mark, Luke, and John. As I spent much time studying the life, death, and resurrection of Jesus, I realized that the Gospels provided a key to understanding all Scripture, from Genesis to Revelation, because the Bible is, indeed, the story of salvation.

One of the Gospel stories that captivated me most was the one that relates the events on the road to Emmaus, found in Luke 24. In this story, we find two disciples of Jesus who are extremely sad because they have lost all hope. They think Jesus is dead and with Him their expectations for the redemption of Israel. All of a sudden, a Stranger starts walking with them. It is Jesus, but they don't recognize Him as they explain to Him what had happened over that fateful weekend.

It is in this story that Jesus explains how to interpret Scripture. He says to them: " 'O foolish men and slow of heart to believe in all that the prophets have spoken! Was it not necessary for the Christ to suffer these things and to enter into His glory?' Then beginning with Moses and with all the prophets, He explained to them the things concerning Himself in all the Scriptures" (Luke 24:25–27). The verb *to explain* (from the Greek *diermēneuō*) is a verb that contains the root word for *hermeneutics,* which in English identifies the methodology of interpreting a biblical text. In this passage, Jesus provides the best interpretive rule: all the Law of Moses and the prophets are about Him.

The resurrected Christ then appears to the rest of the disciples and repeats this hermeneutical principle: "Now He said to them, 'These are My words which I spoke to you while I was still with you, that all things which are written about Me in the Law of Moses and the Prophets and the Psalms must be fulfilled.' Then He opened their minds to understand the Scriptures" (Luke 24:44, 45). "The Law, the Prophets and the Psalms" is the complete formula for the Jewish Scriptures that we have come to call the Old Testament. His disciples knew their Bible, but they did not understand that it was all about Jesus and the salvific act of God through Him. It is possible to read the Scriptures and still have our minds closed. Our minds become open when we understand that all the Law of Moses, the Prophets, and the Psalms are in service to the good news of Jesus Christ.

Matthew takes this understanding very seriously. He writes his Gospel, proposing that Jesus fulfills the Jewish Scriptures. Some scholars believe that the reason this Gospel is placed at the very beginning of the New Testament canon is that it makes the most direct connection between the Old Testament and the life, death, and resurrection of Jesus. As you will find out throughout this booklet, Matthew quotes and alludes to the Jewish Scriptures many, many times and does it deliberately because he believes that Jesus fulfills all Messianic prophecies and all expectations of a Davidic King, and a new and greater Moses.

The Law, the Prophets, and the Psalms contain prophecies about Jesus. These prophecies are promises about what Jesus would accomplish through His perfect life, perfect death, and perfect resurrection. These promises are the basis for the unity between the Old and New Testaments, as Jesus is the climax of salvation history. It is through Him and His accomplishment that we may live with absolute assurance of salvation when we accept Him as our personal Savior.

As we journey together through this booklet, you will frequently find biblical quotations and references, both from the Old and New Testaments. When you do, I invite you to pause your reading and go directly to the Scripture references so that you may receive the full blessings as I did as I came to understand that the whole

Bible is summarized in one word: Jesus.

We are now ready to embark on our journey through Matthew. How exciting! Get your Bible (I use *The New American Standard Bible* version), a pen and paper, and let's put on the hermeneutical glasses that Jesus gave to us: all the Law, the Prophets, and the Psalms are about Him!

The Promise of His Protection

Many years ago, as I was going through a difficult time in my life, one morning I looked out the window of my second-floor condo. There was a thick fog outside, such as I had never seen before. I could make out only the treetops, nothing else. I thought to myself, *This matches the landscape of my heart. This looks like my life. I can't see anything. How am I going to get through this time?* At that moment I felt God speaking to me in my heart. The message was something like this: "I'll get you through it. Just don't let go of my hand."

Wow! I didn't need to see clearly. God would guide me through this difficult time. I was in His grip. A great peace came over me, and at that very moment, I drew a little picture in my devotional book. I still have it. I drew myself as a little girl with my hand in Jesus' hand; dense fog was all around us and only the treetops could be seen above it. That was it! That's the way my life was. But it was enough for me. Somehow, God's message of protection and guidance had reached the core of my being. Matthew starts his Gospel with a similar message.

This Gospel is very special; Matthew really wants us to understand that all the Law, the Prophets, and the Psalms were about Jesus Christ. Matthew quotes the Jewish Scriptures at least forty-seven times, and several of those times he introduces the quotation by explaining that the event fulfilled what the prophet had foretold (see Matthew 1:22; 2:15). What a great view of Scripture! It's all about Jesus! God had a plan all along: Jesus would be the Savior of the world. And now, the mystery of redemption was being revealed.

The Son of David

In the first verse of Matthew, we find a summary of the passages that follows: "the record of the genealogy of Jesus the Messiah, the son of David." It is interesting to notice that Matthew starts his book by referring to Jesus as the son of David. David was the great king of Israel, but as a young boy, he had been a shepherd. You can read about his early life in 1 Samuel, starting with chapter 16. When David became king, God promised him that he would have an everlasting kingdom through his descendants (2 Samuel 7:8–16). His life story is found in 1 and 2 Samuel, 1 and 2 Chronicles, the Psalms, and other places in the Bible.

After hundreds of years had gone by, God gave a prophecy. This prophecy is found in the book of Ezekiel, chapter 34. By this time, Israel as a nation had gone through very difficult times; King David was by then a sweet and distant memory. And this is what the Lord said in Ezekiel 34:2, " 'Son of man, prophesy against the shepherds of Israel. Prophesy and say to those shepherds, "Thus says the LORD GOD, 'Woe, shepherds of Israel who have been feeding themselves! Should not the shepherds feed the flock?' " ' "

God said that those who had been appointed leaders of the people of Israel had not been taking care of them, and that He would come personally to do the job of the shepherd. "Thus says the Lord GOD, 'Behold I Myself will search for My sheep and seek them out. As a shepherd cares for his heard in the day when he is among the scattered sheep, so will I care for My sheep and will deliver them from all the places to which they were scattered on a cloudy and gloomy day' " (Ezekiel 34:11, 12). "A cloudy and gloomy day"—much like my dense fog.

This is great news! God takes care of the feeble and broken. He even looks out for them when they have oppressive leaders!

The true Davidic Shepherd King

How was God going to take care of them? Well, this is where it gets really good! He would do it through a servant who would come in the likeness of David. So, if we go to Ezekiel 34:23, 24, this is what we find: " 'Then I will set over them one shepherd, My servant David, and he will feed them; he will feed them himself and be their shepherd. And I, the LORD, will be their God, and My servant David will be prince among them; I the LORD have spoken.' " The way God was going to shepherd His people was through a descendant of David. Matthew is announcing that Jesus is that Davidic Shepherd King who has come to feed, guide, and protect God's people.

This is the reason why Matthew must establish Jesus' Davidic ancestry from the onset. He wants everyone who reads his book to understand that Jesus is the Anointed One, the Messiah, the descendant of David. Matthew feels so strongly about this emphasis that he divides all the genealogy of Jesus in three groups of fourteen generations. He clearly spells it out: "So all the generations from Abraham to David are fourteen generations; from David to the deportation to Babylon, fourteen generations; and from the deportation to Babylon to the Messiah, fourteen generations" (Matthew 1:17).

Many scholars suggest that Matthew pays so much attention to the number fourteen because the numeric value of the Hebrew consonants in the name *David* add up to fourteen. The main reason for Matthew to focus on Jesus as the son of David is to show that Jesus is the fulfillment of the prophecies regarding the One like David, a descendant of David, who would come to establish the everlasting kingdom of God.

Matthew will also show that Joseph, Jesus' father, is a descendant of David. Matthew 1:20 explains, "When he had considered this, behold, an angel of the Lord appeared to him in a dream, saying, 'Joseph, son of David, do not be afraid to take Mary as your wife.' " This is the only time in the Gospel of Matthew that someone, aside from Jesus, is called son of David. It is designed to show the appropriate lineage of Jesus as the Davidic king. This is why one of Matthew's favorite titles for Jesus is Son of David.

Many narratives in this Gospel emphasize the fact that Jesus is the Son of David. Throughout this Gospel the reader will find kingly and authoritative language. Even the last statement of Jesus conveys the idea of a victory speech: " 'All authority has been given to Me in heaven and on earth' " (Matthew 28:18).

Consider the excitement of the crowd when Jesus comes into the city in a kinglike manner (Matthew 21:1–11). Matthew explains that this is to fulfill what the prophets had said (see Isaiah 62:11; Zechariah 9:9). The crowd was spreading coats and tree branches on the road in front of the coming King, shouting,

> " 'Hosanna to the Son of David;
> BLESSED IS HE WHO COMES IN THE NAME OF THE LORD;
> Hosanna in the highest!' " (Matthew 21:8, 9; cf. Psalm 118:26).

Little did they understand that Jesus' Davidic kingdom was not of this world. His kingdom would be confirmed through His death on the cross (see Matthew 27:37).

Jesus is our Shepherd

It is life changing to realize that God had a salvation plan from the very beginning. When He called David to be the king of Israel, He had in mind the Davidic King who would come much later, a millennium later, to save not just Israel, but everyone who believes in Him.

Perhaps one of the most exciting visualizations of God is the one where we see God as our Shepherd and Protector. When God says in Ezekiel 34 that He would personally come to feed His sheep, protect them, and defend them, and that He would accomplish that through the new David (meaning Jesus), we capture a glimpse of God's love and zeal for us. He is the one who fights for us; He is the one who looks out for us. Jesus is my Shepherd King. He defends me from my foes and from those who oppress me. In the case of Israel, He would defend them from their own leaders, who no longer wanted to care for nor protect the sheep.

When I find myself in a difficult situation that makes me anxious, I visualize myself as a little lamb in Jesus' bosom and recite Psalm 23. David wrote this psalm at the time when he realized that God was the only One who could give him rest, the only One who could guide him, feed him, and protect him. Let's join David in his well-known prayer and song as we envision green pastures and waters of rest. We are His sheep, tired and in need of refreshment. Jesus takes us in His arms:

> The LORD is my shepherd,
> I shall not want.
> He makes me lie down in green pastures;
> He leads me beside quiet waters.
> He restores my soul (Psalm 23:1–3).

May Jesus, the Davidic Shepherd King, restore your soul and give you true rest.

The Promise of His Blessing

OK! Ready for more? We continue with another important name in the ancestry of Jesus—Abraham. Matthew mentions Abraham right after he mentions David in his opening statement (Matthew 1:1). Abraham was the recipient of God's covenant, recorded in the first book of the Bible. In Genesis 12:2–4, God promised Abram (later on God changed his name to Abraham) that all the families of the earth would be blessed through his descendants. You may read the rest of the covenant in Genesis, chapters 12 and 15.

In Matthew 1:1, the author explains that Jesus is a descendant of Abraham, and throughout his Gospel, he reminds the reader that everyone (all the families on the earth) is included in the kingdom of heaven. There are times in our lives when we need to be reminded that we are included, too, that we are not outsiders. If you ever felt that the message of the good news was for everyone except you, Matthew wants to set the record straight—it is for you!

Blessing for all

Matthew starts his inclusive message by listing four women in the genealogy of Jesus; we will call them the great-grandmothers of Jesus. These four great-grandmothers of Jesus are foreigners (some explicitly, others implicitly), who eventually became an integral part of Israel. The first one is Tamar (Matthew 1:3), who posed as a prostitute; you can find her story in Genesis 38. The second great-grandmother is Rahab, a prostitute (Matthew 1:5); you might want to read her fascinating story in Joshua, chapters 2 and 6. The third woman is Ruth, a widow looking for a husband, who lay down at the feet of a man, hoping he would take her as his wife. Her story is found in the book that bears her name, the book of Ruth.

By now you are probably wondering about Matthew's common sense; why would he specifically pick these women? Well, each one of them teaches us something very important about the salvation that would come from Jesus. It gets even more interesting: the fourth and final woman in this genealogy is Bathsheba (Matthew 1:6). David committed adultery with her and then killed her husband in order to cover up his sin. "Jesse was the father of David the king. David was the father of Solomon by Bathsheba who had been the wife of Uriah" (verses 5, 6). This great-grandmother of Jesus will be our focus in this chapter. Her story is found in 2 Samuel, starting from chapter 11.

Bathsheba

Not long ago, I was sitting with a young adult, talking about her future, and she asked me if God could bless her even though she had not done everything according to what she now believes God wanted her to do. She asked me: "Can God bless me with a good marriage even if I have not done things God's way?" I answered with the story of Bathsheba.

You might be thinking, *David again?* Well, David married Bathsheba, and she was an outsider, the wife of a Hittite (the Hittites were one of the seven nations displaced by Israel; see Joshua 3:10). In order to understand the inclusivity of God's blessings, we need to start from the beginning of her story.

The book of 1 Samuel talks about David's journey between his anointment and his appointment as the king. Many of us go through periods in our lives when we are "in between." We feel called by God, we know God anointed us for a role in His kingdom, but we have not yet been appointed to that role. David spent most of his time during this period in caves, so I call it "Cave 101" because that's what it truly was—David was enrolled in God's school. This is a time in which you learn much about yourself and your God, and you find that He is gracious beyond your wildest expectations.

Second Samuel finds David in the high point of his life. In 2 Samuel 5, he becomes king over all of Israel, and in chapter 6, he moves the ark of the covenant, a very important symbol of God's presence with His people, to Jerusalem. In chapter 7, David makes plans to build a temple, and God makes a covenant with him:

> " ' "I took you from the pasture, from following the sheep, to be ruler over My people Israel. . . .
>
> " ' "I will give you rest from all your enemies. The LORD also declares to you that the LORD will make a house for you.
>
> " ' "When your days are complete and you lie down with your fathers, I will raise up your descendant after you, who will come forth from you, and I will establish his kingdom.
>
> " ' "He shall build a house for My name, and I will establish the throne of his kingdom forever.
>
> " ' "I will be a father to him and he will be a son to Me. . . .
>
> " ' "Your house and your kingdom shall endure before Me forever; your throne shall be established forever" ' " (2 Samuel 7:8, 11–16).

Everything is going better than anyone could imagine.

And then it happened.

In chapter 11, everyone is going out to battle, except David. David stays home. In the evening, he arises from his bed, walks on the roof, and sees a woman bathing. She is very beautiful. And David is the king, and maybe he thinks he is above God's moral laws. Upon inquiry, he is told that she is the wife of Uriah the Hittite. But he doesn't care; he is king. David sends messengers, takes her, and has sex with her. And then—soap opera style—she becomes pregnant.

David, like many of us, instead of repenting immediately, tries to hide his sin. He calls her husband back from battle and tells him to go sleep with his wife. Uriah refuses because the rest of David's soldiers are on the battlefield. David finds himself in big trouble. Bathsheba's husband is still loyal to King David, and David cannot convince him to put aside his duty. David thinks that he has only two choices: the first one is to convince Uriah to sleep with Bathsheba; the second one is to get rid of Uriah. Since the first choice is not working, David resorts to his second choice.

You may read this incredible story in 2 Samuel 11, starting from verse 14. Uriah is placed at the front of the battle, where he is killed. Verse 26 says that the wife of Uriah hears that her husband is dead, and she mourns her husband. When the time of mourning is over, David sends for her, and she becomes his wife and bears him a son. But what David does, says the last verse of this chapter, is evil in the sight of the Lord.

The prophet Nathan comes to David in 2 Samuel 12 and tells him a parable (a story told on two levels). He tells the king a story about a rich man who had many lambs, and a poor man who had only one. The rich man takes the one lamb from the poor man. David, thinking that the prophet is giving him a case to solve, burns with anger and tells him that this man deserves to die! Death penalty! At that moment, in a climactic statement, Nathan announces, " 'You are the man!' " (verse 7). Then, following the charge, he gives the verdict—the child will die; David will not.

Blessings

Then something amazing happens that demonstrates to all of us that God's amazing grace is greater than any detours we may have taken in our lives. You know what I am talking about, don't you, the detours that we take by leaving the right path, which lead us into big trouble? Verse 24 says that David comforts his wife Bathsheba and has sex with her, and she gives birth to a son. He names him Solomon. And the Lord loves him.

Can you believe it? How could God bless David and Bathsheba by giving them a son who was the wisest man that ever lived? Why wouldn't God choose any other one of David's wives? What kind of lesson is this? The heir to the throne comes from the sinful union? Isn't this outrageous? Yes, it is outrageous grace. This is the answer for the young adult who was asking me the question mentioned at the beginning of this chapter. It is also the answer for me. And it is the answer for you. On the cross, Jesus purchased the right to bless us in spite of what we have done. He was pierced for our transgressions and crushed for our iniquities. Furthermore, the punishment for our peace was upon Him, and by His stripes we are healed (Isaiah 53:5). May you bask in His grace today!

And so it goes; Bathsheba becomes the great-grandmother of Jesus. Jesus is the descendant of David and Solomon, who establishes the kingdom forever according to the covenant of God with David in 2 Samuel 7.

Blessings for you and me

The great-grandmothers of Jesus remind us that *all nations, all people, everyone* will be blessed through Jesus Christ. Everyone is included in the kingdom of heaven. At the end of the Gospel of Matthew, we are reminded to go out and preach to *all nations.* "And Jesus came up and spoke to them, saying, 'All authority has been given to Me in heaven and on earth. Go therefore and make disciples of all the nations' " (Matthew 28:19, 20).

The genealogy of Jesus reminds us that there are no outsiders in the kingdom of God. Perhaps this is the reason why Matthew is the only Gospel writer to record the visit of the Magi (Matthew 2:1–12). They were not Jews, and yet they were looking for the King of the Jews to worship Him. They had seen His star. God communicated with them, even though they would not have been considered insiders.

Everyone is blessed through Jesus—Abraham's descendant and even those of us who have taken great detours away from the path of righteousness in our lives. God's grace is greater than our detours. No matter where you have been or what you have done, at the very moment you turn your face toward Jesus Christ, the divine GPS reroutes your path to take you toward your divine destination (I would like to redefine GPS as grace positioning system, instead of global positioning system).

Join me in repeating David's prayer recorded in Psalm 51 when he repented from his sin with Bathsheba:

> Wash me, and I shall be whiter than snow.
> Make me to hear joy and gladness. . . .
> Hide Your face from my sins
> And blot out all my iniquities.
> Create in me a clean heart, O God,
> And renew a steadfast spirit within me (Psalm 51:7–10).

Yes, Lord, create a clean heart in me that seeks *only* after You! I want to be Your child, after Your own heart.

The Promise of His Presence

A s you have probably realized by now, most of the main theological themes proposed by Matthew are laid out in the first few chapters of his Gospel. In chapter 1, verse 18, he begins the narrative of the birth of Jesus. And it starts with a problem: the timing of the pregnancy. Mary and Joseph are engaged but not married; this is not the right time for a pregnancy.

I must admit that I have had many questions about God's timing in my life. I have struggled with it. But His answer to me has always been, "Don't be afraid; I am with you." God doesn't always explain His timing, but He always promises His presence. I no longer try to understand because I have come to trust that God knows many things that I don't. I just try to become aware of His presence, particularly when I don't understand His timing.

Back to our story, Joseph and Mary are engaged but not living together. Joseph learns that Mary is pregnant, and he knows that he is not the father. He chooses to secretly divorce her (this was required to break an engagement at that time) to avoid more problems. While he is pondering these things, an angel of the Lord appears with a message. Before we go on, let me share something with you.

Matthew is a skilled and deliberate theologian. He arranges his material carefully to impact the reader in powerful ways; he gives his message to his audience in a very effective way. The number five is very important to his Jewish audience because of the five books of the Law (the Torah). Matthew carefully arranges his material in groups of five. We call them the five discourses. And it is important to notice that even the infancy of Jesus is narrated in five episodes. Each episode is constructed around an Old Testament prophecy:

the birth, the Magi, the flight to Egypt, Herod slaughtering babies, and Jesus growing up in Nazareth.

In this fivefold infancy narrative, God is in absolute control. He sends His angel, sometimes in a dream (as was expected in that culture when deities communicated with humans), and He directs and orchestrates each important move for Joseph, Mary, and Jesus. In the five narratives, everyone except Herod is guided by God. Still, Matthew manages to talk about five dreams, as he talks of two dreams in the last episode. The fact that God is so willing to communicate with humans to guide them in difficult situations has always brought much comfort to my soul.

God has far more skills and resources than hundreds of people with PhDs in communication! And when I decide to do God's will, it becomes His responsibility to reveal it to me. He doesn't hide it or play a treasure hunt with me; neither does He laugh devilishly when I don't figure it out. No! He sends me all kinds of messages through His Word, spiritual leaders, open and closed doors, and my sense of peace (see Isaiah 55:12). He guides me through paths of righteousness for His name's sake (Psalm 23).

Immanuel: God with us

Now back to our story. The first of the five episodes is the actual birth of Jesus. Matthew 1:20 informs the reader that an angel of the Lord appeared to Joseph in a dream. The angel calls Joseph " 'son of David.' " As it was explained in the first chapter, this is the only time that anyone, other than Jesus, is called son of David in this Gospel, and it establishes Jesus' Davidic ancestry. The angel announces that Mary will bear a Son; His name would be *Jesus* (Yeshua, Joshua), which means "Yahweh (the LORD) saves" (verse 21).

In the next two verses (22, 23), we encounter the first Matthean prophetic "formula." "Now all this took place to fulfill what was spoken by the Lord through the prophet: 'BEHOLD, THE VIRGIN SHALL BE WITH CHILD AND SHALL BEAR A SON, AND THEY SHALL

CALL HIS NAME IMMANUEL,' which translated means, 'GOD WITH US.'" This quote comes from Isaiah 7:14. In Isaiah, chapter 7, Ahaz, king of Judah, is in trouble. The kings of Aram and Israel are coming to war against him, and Ahaz and his people are very afraid (Isaiah 7:2). The Lord sends Isaiah to talk to Ahaz, and he finds him surveying the water reservoir, a smart thing to do in this situation because Jerusalem didn't have good water supply. Isaiah brings to Ahaz the promise of God's presence and tries to keep him from making alliances with other military powers. Isaiah tells the king not to be afraid. Then the Lord tells Ahaz to ask Him for a sign, and it would be given to him. But Ahaz refuses to ask the Lord for help.

Nevertheless, God decides to give Ahaz a sign so that he would always remember that God had offered him the comfort of His presence in this difficult time. A maiden would bear a son, and she would call him *Immanuel,* which means "with us God." In other words, God is with us. Can you imagine? *God* is with us. God *is* with us. God is *with* us. God is with *us!* The promise of His presence is given in one way or another in every book of the Bible. It is the most important promise offered to humanity. God, who created us, is with us!

Matthew proposes that this prophecy is ultimately fulfilled in Jesus. I believe that God really proved that He is with us when He came to save us. The angel said to Joseph that the baby's name would be Jesus, because He would save His people from their sins. Hanging on the cross, Immanuel cried out to God, " 'ELI, ELI, LAMA SABACHTHANI?' that is, 'MY GOD, MY GOD, WHY HAVE YOU FORSAKEN ME?' " (Matthew 27:46).

It is startling to notice that the same "El" in Immanu*el*, is the "El" Jesus is crying out to when He says "Eli, Eli" (My God, My God). Immanuel was abandoned in our place so that we may never be. He suffered the penalty of our sins as a Parent who was willing to take the death penalty for a crime committed by His child. This is the climax of God's presence: Immanuel hanging on the cross.

God is with us

The promise of God's presence is another *inclusio* in the Gospel of Matthew. An *inclusio* is like a narrative sandwich: the narrative begins and ends with the same topic. Matthew starts his narrative about Jesus with "Immanuel: God with us," and he ends his Gospel with Jesus announcing, " 'I am with you always, even to the end of the age' " (Matthew 28:20). This is God's promise to us: He will never leave us. When Adam sinned, God gave him the promise of redemption (Genesis 3:15), and when this earth is re-created, we will finally be with God forever (Revelation 21:3, 4).

The entire Bible, from beginning to end, is about the plan of redemption God made in order to save us so that we could be with Him forever, exactly as He had planned when He created us in His image. From Genesis to Revelation, we go full circle, which was made possible through Jesus' suffering on the cross. When we decided to run away from Him, God refused to leave us. He wouldn't go through eternity without us.

May the promise of His presence be yours in your soul today and every day, until we see Immanuel face-to-face when He comes to take us home (Matthew 24:29–31). And if you ever struggle with His timing, remember the promise of His presence. He says to you, "Don't be afraid: I am Immanuel, and I am with you." Yes, you are in His grip, and He won't let you go.

The Promise of His Guidance

E ven though Matthew is writing to a predominantly Jewish audience, he desires to emphasize the inclusivity of Jesus' mission. Jesus came for all—both Jew and Gentile. This, in itself, was a fulfillment of the covenant with Abraham in Genesis 12: " 'And in you all the families of the earth will be blessed' " (verse 3). I am *so* thankful for this covenant because it includes *me*! I am part of all the families of the earth!

The inclusivity of the kingdom of heaven is portrayed by Matthew throughout his Gospel. One example is the story of how Jesus marveled at the faith of a centurion (Matthew 8:5–13). Jesus said, " 'Truly I say to you, I have not found such great faith with anyone in Israel' " (verse 10). Matthew then adds a comment Jesus made that is not recorded by Luke. " 'I say to you that many will come from east and west, and recline at the table with Abraham, Isaac and Jacob in the kingdom of heaven' " (verse 11). And from the east came an interesting group of people to worship the new King of the Jews.

The story of the Magi from the east is recorded only by Matthew. Some question the historicity of this account, but the truth is that the early Christian church would never have made up this particular story; a church that opposed the practice of magic and astrology would never have invented such unworthy (in their own eyes) witnesses to the Child Jesus.

Seeking the Child King

Matthew 2:1–12 narrates this exciting and gripping story (take a moment to read it before we go on). Matthew starts the narrative reminding the reader that Jesus (the first character in this story) was born in Bethlehem of Judea. Matthew could have given many designations to this village in order to differentiate it from other places with the same name, but he chooses "Bethlehem of Judea" because this is the tribe and territory of the Davidic kings; King David was from Bethlehem of Judea (cf. 1 Samuel 16). Could this be Jesus, the Davidic King?

The next part of the sentence introduces the second character in this story: Herod the king (Matthew 2:1). This is Herod the Great, an Idumaean client king. He was ruthless: he murdered his wife, three sons, brother-in-law, mother-in-law, and many others, in addition to the babies in Bethlehem. He wanted no competition! And he would stop at nothing to eliminate anybody who might become his rival. He was also known for his building projects, including the rebuilding of the temple in Jerusalem that was completed several years after his death. It is not just in modern times that we find those who would do anything to climb the corporate ladder. Herod, "the king," wanted to make sure his title remained undisturbed. The juxtaposition of Jesus, the Davidic King, with Herod, the client king, already tastes like trouble.

The third group introduced in Matthew 2:1 is the "magi from the east." The Magi are a priestly caste of astrologers and magicians from Persia or Babylon, usually trusted advisors to the king (see Daniel 1, 2). They arrived in Jerusalem, the capital of the Jews, asking a question. " 'Where is He who has been born King of the Jews? For we saw His star in the east and have come to worship Him' " (Matthew 2:2).

Now we have a problem. They are asking about the King of the Jews who was born, and King Herod hears about it. The juxtaposition of the two different responses to the news is striking: the pagan Magi have come to worship; Herod the king, and all Jerusalem with him, are troubled (Matthew 2:3). Talk about a paradox! It gets even worse! The chief priests and scribes, the religious elite, are consulted by Herod and seem to be part of his group; at least they

THE PROMISE OF HIS GUIDANCE

do not follow along with the Magi in their quest for the Messiah. They have the biblical knowledge, but not the worshipful spirit! That hurts! We can study the Bible, know the prophecies by heart, and still miss Jesus.

Before we go into the prophecy the priests and scribes quoted back to Herod, let's analyze another "Magi" who had given a prophecy of a star that would rise from Judea. I am talking about Balaam; you might remember him because he had the unusual experience of dialoguing with his donkey (Numbers 22:22–35). The similarities with the Matthean Magi are striking: Balaam is a non-Israelite wizard from the east (called a *magos* by Philo), who is hired by a wicked king to curse the people of God. But instead, he blesses them and gives a prophecy of a King who would rise from Israel and a star that would come forth from Jacob (Numbers 24:17).

Some believe that Balaam's prophecy is what inspired the Magi from the east to look for a special star. Nevertheless, the Magi from the east don't seem familiar with the specific prophecy of the place where the Messiah would be born. So, they come to Jerusalem asking, "Where is He?" God uses many different ways to communicate with us and guide us to Him. And then He takes us directly to the Scriptures for the complete revelation of who He is and what His will is for us.

A tale of two kings

Herod does not ask the chief priests and scribes where the King of the Jews would be born. He asked them where the Messiah was to be born (Matthew 2:4). The religious leaders answer, " 'In Bethlehem of Judea.' " Matthew comments,

"This is what has been written by the prophet:
'AND YOU, BETHLEHEM, LAND OF JUDAH,
ARE BY NO MEANS LEAST AMONG THE LEADERS OF JUDAH;

• 29 •

FOR OUT OF YOU SHALL COME FORTH A RULER
WHO WILL SHEPHERD MY PEOPLE ISRAEL' " (Matthew
2:5, 6).

This quotation fuses a prophecy from Micah 5:2, given seven centuries earlier with a Davidic passage found in 2 Samuel 5:2.

Furthermore, Matthew reverses a concept in Micah 5:2, calling Bethlehem " ' "*by no means least* among the leaders of Judah" ' " (Matthew 2:6; compare with Micah 5:2, " 'Bethlehem Ephrathah, / *Too little to be* among the clans of Judah' "), because Bethlehem was now the birthplace of Jesus, the Davidic King (emphases added). Can you believe that God knew the exact place where Jesus would be born hundreds of years before? And Joseph and Mary didn't even live there—they lived in Nazareth. God even knew that they would be on a trip to Bethlehem because of a census. And because Joseph and Mary were from the Davidic line, they had to go to Bethlehem, where David was born, and then—OK, you get the picture. But let me just get this off my chest: I am truly *amazed* at God's knowledge of the future! Aren't you?

Herod secretly calls the Magi and finds out from them the exact time the star had appeared (Matthew 2:7), which was probably about two years earlier, because he eventually orders all Bethlehem babies under two years killed to eliminate any possible competition (Matthew 2:16–18). Ruthless! He tried to pretend to be interested in worshiping Jesus (Matthew 2:7, 8), but God eventually unmasked him in a dream He sent to the Magi, and they never saw Herod again (Matthew 2:12).

Eureka! They found Him!

The Magi were on their way to Bethlehem, and when they saw the star, "They rejoiced exceedingly with great joy" (Matthew 2:10). How many adjective and superlatives can you add? They rejoiced exceedingly with great joy! Did I say they were joyful? I love it! You know those times when words are not enough, when you just cry, jump, dance, or fall on your knees? When you get just a glimpse of God's grace that surpasses words? Well, this was one of those times. I love the Greek word for "great" joy. It is *megalēn*. Do you recognize the word *mega*? Megaphone, megachurch, big, big, mega! Well, this is what you can call megajoy!

They eventually came into the house; they saw the Child Jesus with Mary, His mother, and they "fell to the ground and worshiped Him" (Matthew 2:11). I would love to have been there! Right there on the ground with them! Worshiping God made flesh! Wow! A mystery that I will study for eternity! They opened their treasures, gold, frankincense, and myrrh. Some find these to be typological gifts: gold for the King of kings, incense for the Priest of priests, and myrrh for the greatest sacrificial Lamb. Through these gifts, God provided for Jesus' family during their flight to Egypt and later life. God was in control and took care of their provision to the smallest detail. He also guided the pagan Magi toward Him in a way they would understand.

Matthew does not again use the title King of the Jews for Jesus until chapter 27, where Jesus is condemned and killed. This title, always spoken by non-Jews in this Gospel, is used again by the governor who interrogates Jesus (verse 11), and it is the legal charge placed on the cross. The Roman charge against Jesus was treason. "And above His head they put up the charge against Him which read, 'THIS IS JESUS THE KING OF THE JEWS' " (Matthew 27:37).

This is another *inclusio* in the Gospel of Matthew, a narrative sandwich. Paradoxically, this title for Jesus is used at the beginning and at the end of the Gospel, highlighting many of the theological themes portrayed in this Gospel, including outsiders coming into the kingdom of heaven and the rejection of Jesus by the Jewish leaders.

Matthew even includes a small section (Matthew 28:11–15), missing in the other Gospels, in which he explains that the elders, who together with the chief priest and scribes formed the Sanhe-drin (the central Jewish authority under Herod), gave a large sum of money to the soldiers to keep quiet about Jesus' resurrection. Then he adds, "And they took the money and did as they had been instructed; and this story was widely spread among the Jews, and is to this day" (Matthew 28:15). There is no doubt that the Matthean community was at odds with the Jewish leaders regarding their belief in Jesus Christ, even though most of them were Jewish Christians.

God guides us

The story of how God reached out to the Gentiles to reveal the birth of Jesus has been celebrated by Western Christianity as the feast of Epiphany. I have a childhood memories, both in Argentina and Uruguay, of leaving my shoes outside my bedroom door so that the wise men, as they passed by, would leave me gifts. Just for fun, the children would leave straw and water for the camels. This cele-bration includes the profound understanding that God reached out to all nations with the good news of the Savior's birth.

I invite you to create a reminder of God's desire to guide you. Cut a star out of cardboard and glue a small mirror in the center of the star (I have one next to me right now). Not only will the star look "shiny" because of the mirror, but every time you look at it, you will see your own face, and you will remember God's commit-ment to communicate and guide *you,* the one in the mirror.

God knows how to reach out to you in a way you understand. If you want to follow Him, He will make sure you understand the way. You have heard it said, "Wise men still seek Him." But the truth is God still seeks them. God still seeks us. God seeks *you,* the one in the mirror. And when you receive God's revelation of Jesus in your life, you will rejoice exceedingly with great joy, with mega-joy!

The Promise of His Perfection

Matthew makes three major proposals throughout his Gospel regarding Jesus' relationship to the Jewish Scriptures, the Old Testament: (1) Jesus fulfills the Messianic prophecies because He is the expected Davidic Ruler (see chapter one), (2) Jesus is the new and greater Moses, and (3) Jesus re-lives Israel's history, and He is victorious where they failed. The third proposal is the focus of this chapter.

In the Jewish Scriptures, Israel is called God's son. Many times God talks about Israel in these terms:

> When Israel was a youth I loved him,
> And out of Egypt I called My son. . . .
> It is I who taught Ephraim to walk,
> I took them in My arms (Hosea 11:1–3).

This was the corporate form of *sonship* presented in the Old Testament. There was also an individual form of *sonship:* that of the king of Israel, the leader and representative of the people of Israel. Therefore, the Davidic kings were also called God's sons. For example, when God speaks to David about his descendant, He declares, " 'I will be a father to him and he will be a son to Me' " (2 Samuel 7:14). The people of Israel (corporately) and the king of Israel (individually) are the two Old Testament precursors of the father/son symbolism we find in the New Testament.

Matthew proposes that Jesus re-lives Israel's history. Therefore, he sometimes quotes verses that relate to Israel and applies them to Jesus. For example, when Matthew narrates the Infant Jesus' escape to Egypt, he cites Hosea 11:1, "This was to fulfill what had been spoken by the Lord through the prophet: 'OUT OF EGYPT I CALLED MY SON' " (Matthew 2:15). This proposal becomes most evident in the Matthean narrative during the temptations of Jesus in the wilderness. To study this exciting story with its full in-depth fulfillment force, read the rest of this chapter with your Bible open in two places: Matthew 4 and Deuteronomy 6–8.

Jesus versus Satan

This story is found in other Gospels as well, but Matthew makes the most direct connection with the Old Testament events by repeating key words that were used in Deuteronomy. Let's start with his introduction to the three temptations described in Matthew 4:1, 2. "Then Jesus was led up by the Spirit into the wilderness to be tempted by the devil. And after He had fasted forty days and forty nights, He then became hungry." Now, let's go to Deuteronomy 8:2, 3. " 'You shall remember all the way which the LORD your God has led you in the wilderness these forty years, that He might humble you, testing you, to know what was in your heart, whether you would keep His commandments or not. He humbled you and let you be hungry.' "

Take a moment to observe the same words present in both passages—there are many! Matthew has set the stage for us to remember Israel's journey in the wilderness, the forty years, the leading of God, the test, the hunger, etc.

The devil tempts Jesus with an if statement: " 'If You are the Son of God, command that these stones become bread' " (Matthew 4:3). Israel had struggled with lack of food in the wilderness; now Jesus re-lives this experience and responds, " 'It is written, "MAN SHALL NOT LIVE ON BREAD ALONE, BUT ON EVERY WORD THAT PROCEEDS OUT OF THE MOUTH OF GOD" ' " (Matthew 4:4). This is a passage written about Israel's history. " 'He humbled you and let you be hungry, and fed you with manna which you did not know, nor did your fathers know, that He might make you understand that man does not live by bread alone, but man lives by everything that proceeds out of the mouth of the LORD' " (Deuteronomy 8:3; see Matthew 4:4).

Then the devil gets smart and starts quoting Scripture himself (be aware that not everyone who quotes Scripture is speaking for God). Matthew 4:5, 6, tells how Satan quotes Psalm 91:11, 12, as he tempts Jesus to throw himself down from the pinnacle of the temple in order to show that he is the Son of God. To respond to this second temptation, Jesus goes back to Israel's history again by quoting from Deuteronomy 6:16, " 'You shall not put the LORD your God to the test' " (see Matthew 4:7). Then the devil shows Jesus all the kingdoms of the world and their glory (I would really like to know what software he used) and offers them all to Jesus if only He would do one little thing: worship the devil.

This was a temptation to bypass the cross, as if salvation could have been achieved any other way. Israel had been tempted to find its own way and worship other gods. Then Jesus tells him, " 'Go, Satan!' " in other words—get lost! (Matthew 4:10). The Greek word (*hypage*) is an imperative that means "away with you." Jesus is not just telling the devil that this dialogue is over. He is telling him to go fly a kite or take a hike! This kind of colloquial language is even sharper because of the use of the word *Satan,* which literally means "enemy."

Jesus doesn't hesitate to unmask Satan whenever he tempts Him to bypass the cross. He even calls his friend Peter, " 'Satan' " when he tries to do the same (Matthew 16:22, 23). Jesus' final response comes from Deuteronomy 6:13. " 'You shall fear only the LORD your God; and you shall worship Him' " (see Matthew 4:10). Then the devil leaves Jesus.

This is not the last time that Jesus encountered "if You are" type of temptations. Even while hanging on the cross, He hears, " 'If You are the Son of God, come down from the cross' " (Matthew 27:40). By now, the reader is fully aware of the source of such temptations: it's the enemy! And Jesus knows that.

Sometimes, we don't know. The devil is quite skilled at asking us to prove ourselves to God and to others. "If you are a child of God, you shouldn't be going through this hardship," or "If you were a child of God, you wouldn't have behaved this way; you have gone too far." But that is *not* the truth. The truth is Jesus, and the name *Jesus* means "Yahweh saves" (see Matthew 1:21). I know that He has saved me, so I can boldly say, "Away with you, Satan!"

Jesus' victory for me

Matthew's proposal that Jesus re-lives Israel's history and is victorious in everything they failed in has brought great peace to my soul. The fact that Jesus lived a perfect life in my place, and that He died a perfect death in my place is the source of assurance of my salvation. When God sees me, He doesn't see my record—no, no, no! He sees Jesus' perfect righteousness in my place. I can choose the worst week in my life, and I know it is covered by Jesus' perfect righteousness.

When I accept Jesus' victory in my place, and I ask him to be my personal Savior and cleanse me from my sin through His blood, God sees Jesus, not me, and I am accepted through *the Beloved!* Wow! Whenever I try talking to God about a sin of mine hidden in Christ, God invariably responds with a question, "What sin?"

My dear friend, Matthew proposed to Israel that their history was hidden in Christ. Jesus re-lived and rewrote their history. I invite you to believe the same. Your story is His story. Accept Jesus Christ as your personal Savior, as the perfect Lamb of God who was slain in your place. Now live in the joy and assurance of your salvation. And when Satan tries to tell you otherwise, in Jesus' name, tell him to take a hike!

The Promise of His Provision

Have you ever felt like an outsider? As a Latino woman, I have sometimes felt the sting of not belonging, the glances that speak louder than words. Sometimes it may be my accent, sometimes simply because I am a female pastor. Overall, I have felt accepted in most circles even though at times I became painfully aware that I was not considered an insider.

The Gospel of Matthew brings good news to both Gentiles and Jews, as the narrative reveals that those outside of the Jewish religious boundaries are included along with the Jews in the kingdom of God. One of the ways in which Matthew presents this good news is through a deliberate narrative development using the topic of bread (following Mark's narrative proposal, see Mark 6:30–8:26).

The bread plot that we will examine together is found in Matthew 14:13–15:39. Please take a moment to read these verses. Matthew uses the two feeding accounts (five thousand [14:13–21] and four thousand [15:32–39]) as *framing episodes* and the story of the Syrophoenician woman (15:21–28) as the center of the material they frame. Think of these three episodes as enacted parables—teachings of Jesus that carry deep spiritual insights beyond feeding and healing.

Bread for five thousand

The narrative starts with Jesus going to a secluded place. In this remote place, He sees a large crowd and feels compassion for them and heals their sick (Matthew 14:14). When evening comes, the disciples notice a problem and mention it to Jesus: it is a *desolate* place, the hour is late, and these people need to eat (verse 15). The

Jewish reader would have two very important expectations in mind—the new Davidic Shepherd King would *feed* the sheep (Ezekiel 34:23, 24), and the new and greater Moses should be able to feed the people in a *desolate* place, just as Moses had done during the Exodus (certain words are often repeated throughout the narrative to provide an Old Testament setting).

Exodus 16 tells the story of the time when the people of Israel faced their need for food. This is a fascinating account because many themes in this story will be applied by Jesus to Himself (see John 6:1–58). God provides manna for them, bread that rains from heaven. The people of Israel are being trained by God to trust that He would provide for their needs. Now Jesus is in a *desolate* place with no food and a large crowd. Would He be able to provide bread as well? The disciples don't seem to think so, because they propose that Jesus send the crowd away that they might buy food for themselves (Matthew 14:15). Jesus has other plans.

"But Jesus said to them, 'They do not need to go away; you give them *something* to eat!' " (verse 16, emphasis in original). The disciples answer that they only have five loaves of bread and two fish. Jesus tells them to bring it to Him (verses 17, 18); then He orders everyone to sit down (verse 19). The Gospel of Mark tells us that they sat down in groups of fifties and hundreds (Mark 6:40), just as in the time of the Mosaic camp (see Exodus 18:21). Jesus then does something very important and unexpected—He multiplies the bread.

There are four verbs that the reader will re-encounter later on in the bread plot: He *takes* the loaves, He *blesses* them, He *breaks* the loaves, and He *gives* them to the disciples. The disciples then give the bread to the crowds (Matthew 14:19). The conclusion says, "They all ate and were satisfied. They picked up what was left over of the broken pieces, twelve full baskets. There were about five thousand men who ate, besides women and children" (verses 20, 21).

The setting of this enacted parable is given in sociopolitical and religious terms, which are mainly found in the words and numbers used. The number five and the number twelve were representative of the Jewish culture: five was the number of the books in the Law (Torah), and there were twelve tribes in Israel. In this story, there are five loaves of bread, five thousand men fed, and twelve full baskets left. There is enough bread for the Jews to be *satisfied,* and there are leftovers, a full basket for each tribe. The Greek word used for baskets in this story is *kophinoi,* a type of basket usually associated with the Jews. When everyone is fed and satisfied, Jesus gives orders for them to go to *the other side.*

Have you ever wondered if there is enough for you? When I was a little girl, my dad was a church administrator. Once or twice a year, we would go to collect the tithes and offerings of church members who lived far from church congregations. Once we had to go to the mountains where a woman owned a hotel. At that time, I had been saving pennies and nickels to buy a bicycle. When my parents and I got to the hotel, she had us sit down at a table. I could barely see above it. Then she brought a heap of money like I had never seen before (nor have I ever since, so it seems). She started stacking the money on the table in little piles and designating their purpose out loud: this pile is for evangelism, this is for church budget, this is tithe, etc. I was sure there would be a pile for me.

When she had finished and there were no more coins to designate, I thought the time had come to do something about it. With all the volume my little lungs could master, I yelled in utter desperation, "And for my bicycle?" I'm going to have a talk with this woman in heaven, because I don't remember that she gave me anything. My loud cry became a metaphorical saying in my family. Whenever someone wanted something for themselves, such as food, money, or attention, we would say, "And for my bicycle?"

There have been a few times when I have asked God this question throughout my life. In the times of Jesus, some people wondered whether there was enough for them. They lived on the other side of the lake (Matthew 14:22). The *other side* is usually a loaded phrase in the Gospels; it means "outsiders."

The breakthrough

Somehow, the storm detours the disciples from Jesus' orders, and they find themselves back in Jewish territory, in Gennesaret (Matthew 14:34). Some Pharisees and scribes come to Jesus from Jerusalem and start talking with Him about bread. They ask Him about His disciples and why they don't wash their hands before they eat (Matthew 15:1, 2). Jesus then engages in teaching about clean and unclean, about what *really* defiles a person (verses 3–20).

After discussing what is really unclean and defiling, Jesus crosses over to unclean territory. Jesus enters Tyre and Sidon, pagan territory that carried a long history of antagonism for the people of Israel (verse 21; see 1 Kings 16:31, 32). Jesus is now clearly in Gentile territory, and a Canaanite woman from that region comes asking Jesus, the Son of David, for mercy (verses 21, 22). The woman implores for her demon-possessed daughter—"and for my bicycle?" Is there something for me, Jesus?

The disciples, feeling uncomfortable, ask Jesus to send her away (verse 23). She takes the place of the crowd in the previous feeding. When approached by this woman, Jesus explains to her that He was sent to the lost sheep of Israel (see Ezekiel 34:23, 24). And when she keeps asking for help, Jesus speaks to her in a riddle about bread. "And He answered and said, 'It is not good to take the children's bread and throw it to the dogs' " (Matthew 15:26). Mark adds, " 'Let the children be satisfied first' " (Mark 7:27). *Satisfied* is a key word present in both feedings.

The woman responds to the riddle and does not ask for the children's bread or for the first place. She asks for the humble place of a little dog that eats bread from the children's leftovers. She proposes crumbs. The children can be satisfied first with the bread; all she wants is the crumbs of bread that fall from the table. Jesus commends her faith and heals her daughter.

Many scholars believe this is *the breakthrough event* in the Gospel of Matthew. This is where the reader realizes that there are no outsiders in the kingdom of heaven. This is when we start to get a glimpse of the inclusivity of Jesus' mission. Could it be? Could it really be true that I am included? Another feeding follows, and this time, the numbers have changed.

Bread for four thousand

This time it is Jesus who brings up the people's need for food; the disciples simply resist (Matthew 15:32, 33). Jesus asks them how many loaves they have, and they answer " 'seven' " (verse 34). The number of fish is not given.

Jesus directs the people to sit down on the ground, and once again we encounter four verbs: He *takes* the seven loaves of bread, He *gives thanks* (instead of blessing them as He did in the first feeding), He *breaks* the loaves, and He *gives* them to the disciples, who give them to the people (verses 35, 36). The report is the same as in the previous feeding, only the numbers and the word used for baskets have changed. "And they all ate and were satisfied, and they picked up what was left over of the broken pieces, seven large baskets full. And those who ate were four thousand men, besides women and children" (verses 37, 38). Yes, they all *ate* and were *satisfied* and there were leftovers.

In this story, the numbers have changed from five and twelve to seven and four. These numbers represent those on *the other side.* The number four is used to highlight people who come from the four corners of the earth, from the four cardinal points. In the non-Jewish/Gentile geographical setting, seven symbolizes one basket per pagan nation displaced by Israel in the land of Canaan. "When He had destroyed seven nations in the land of Canaan, He distributed their land as an inheritance" (Acts 13:19). Seven is used in other Hellenistic settings, such as the choosing of the seven deacons with Greek names in Acts 6:1–6 in response to the accusation of the Hellenistic Jews. The word for baskets is *spyrides* (Matthew 15:37), as opposed to *kophinoi* in the previous feeding (Matthew

14:20). The first word is befitting of a Gentile audience, while the latter was regularly associated with the Jews.

Jews and non-Jews alike have been provided for. Jesus has fed them all as the Davidic Prince (Ezekiel 34:23, 24). Just as Moses had done (Exodus 16), He has also miraculously fed large crowds in a *desolate* place. Every single one is now satisfied. It is time to solve the bread riddle.

Bread riddle solved

The passage that unravels the mystery of the bread riddle starts as follows: "While they were eating, Jesus *took* some bread, and after a *blessing,* He *broke* it and *gave* it to the disciples, and said, 'Take, eat; this is My body' " (Matthew 26:26, emphasis added). The mystery is revealed! The bread is His broken body! This revelation is preceded by verbs now recognized by the reader—He took, He blessed or thanked, He broke, and He gave as He had done in both feedings.

The mystery is solved: the sacrifice of Jesus is for all! There is enough for children and dogs, for the five thousand and the four thousand; there are small baskets (*kophinoi*) and there are large baskets (*spyrides*) filled with broken bread. All can be satisfied with the provision made on the Cross. And there are leftovers for the twelve tribes of Israel and the seven pagan nations. This is truly good news. The scope of the good news is greater than anyone had imagined. There is enough bread for those on one side of the lake as there is for those on the other side.

The Gospel of John makes this striking proposal through a lengthy interaction between Jesus and the people after the feeding of the five thousand (John 6:26–58). In this conversation, Jesus reveals that He is the Bread of Life and that He is the true Manna, which comes down from heaven. " 'I am the bread of life. Your fathers ate the manna in the wilderness, and they died. This is the bread which comes down out of heaven, so that one may eat of it and not die. I am the living bread that came down out of heaven; if anyone eats of this bread, he will live forever; and the bread also which I will give for the life of the world is My flesh' " (John 6:48–51). Oh, the beauty of reading Scripture in the light of Jesus and Jesus in light of the Scriptures! Jesus is the real Manna! Jesus is the real Passover Lamb!

There are days in which we might wonder if there is enough for us—to wonder "and for my bicycle?" Sometimes, the devil tempts us to believe that we are not included in God's salvation. We may reason, "Yes, Jesus is the Savior of the world, but I may have gone too far." Remember the Bread! Enough for everyone on this side and the *other side.* Enough bread for those who seem to have it all together and those who don't. Leftovers for the children and *the dogs.* His grace *is* sufficient. There is enough for your bicycle and for mine. May you live in the abundance of recognizing that Jesus' broken body purchased you and that there is plenty for everyone. Eat the Bread!

Let's pray together. How about the Lord's prayer?

> " 'Our Father who is in heaven,
> Hallowed be Your name.
> Your kingdom come.
> Your will be done,
> On earth as it is in heaven.
> Give us this day *our daily bread*' " (Matthew 6:9–11,
>   emphasis added).

Amen.

The Promise of His Supremacy

One of Matthew's most prominent proposals throughout his Gospel is that Jesus is the new and greater Moses. There was a prophecy recorded in Moses' own words: " 'The LORD your God will raise up for you a prophet like me from among you, from your countrymen, you shall listen to him' " (Deuteronomy 18:15). Many believe that this prophecy indicates that a series of spokesmen would be provided for Israel. This prophecy is also the basis for an important Messianic expectation—a new and greater Moses would come to guide God's people in their understanding of the Torah (Law).

Matthew proposes that Jesus is the new and greater Moses. Many narrative tools are used in this Gospel to make this point clearly and boldly. The number five was very important to the Jews because the Law was composed of five books. As mentioned in a previous chapter, Matthew divides Jesus' infancy into five narratives, each one alluding to an Old Testament prophecy. More important, Matthew divides his Gospel into five main discourses of Jesus, each one concluding with the phrase "when Jesus had finished . . ." The five discourses are as follows:

1. the kingdom's manifesto (Matthew 5–7),
2. the kingdom's mission (Matthew 10),
3. the kingdom's parables (Matthew 13),
4. the kingdom's community (Matthew 18),
5. and the kingdom's future (Matthew 24, 25).

The kingdom's manifesto is known as the Sermon on the Mount. In this discourse, Jesus teaches His disciples on the mountain in a Moseslike manner. He states clearly the reversal of values proposed in the kingdom of heaven and the blessedness that comes to those who practice them (Matthew 5:1–12). He talks about discipleship and the importance of glorifying God with our lives. Jesus reiterates His intent to fulfill the Law and the Prophets (see verse 17). He also expands the law to a more profound level, where a definition of murder is now extended to include mere anger against a brother (verses 21, 22), and adultery is now defined as lust (verses 27, 28). He replaces those laws that separated people (verses 38, 39).

These expansions and replacements usually have the format "You have heard . . . but I tell you. . . ." He speaks of prayer (Matthew 6:7–15) and the cure for anxiety (verses 25–34). This discourse is the manifesto of the kingdom, outlining the values of the kingdom of heaven. He summarizes the Law and the Prophets with the golden rule (Matthew 7:12).

God's Son is supreme

One of the stories in which we clearly see Matthew's intent in portraying Jesus as the new and greater Moses is the Transfiguration account recorded in Matthew 17:1–8. Jesus took Peter, James, and John up on a high mountain. This account includes many words that remind us of the Old Testament event (Exodus 34:29–35) when Moses went up on a mountain to receive from God the commandments for His people who had entered into a renewed covenant with Him. When Moses came down from being with God, his face was shining, a fact that is mentioned several times in the text.

It is not a surprise that Matthew wants to make sure that his hearers and readers understand that when Jesus is transfigured into His glorious state in front of His three inner circle disciples, His face, not just His garments (see Mark 9:2–10), is shining like the sun (Matthew 17:2).

And lo and behold, Moses and Elijah appear in the scene (Matthew mentions Moses first, unlike Mark; see Mark 9:4) and are talking with Jesus. Moses was the representative of the Law, and

Elijah, of the Prophets. Throughout this Gospel, Matthew proposes that Jesus fulfills the Law and the Prophets, and in this scene we find a climactic portrayal of this proposal—the Law and the Prophets are talking with Jesus. It is a beautiful portrait of the continuum between the Old and the New Testaments. Jesus' mission is informed by the Law and the Prophets; Jesus Himself is informed by Moses and Elijah. This portrait seems so perfect that Peter wants to freeze it for a while. " 'Lord, it is good for us to be here; if You wish, I will make three tabernacles here, one for You, and one for Moses, and one for Elijah' " (Matthew 17:4). It sounds reasonable, doesn't it? Except that Peter's proposal places all three in the same level, as if Jesus, Moses, and Elijah all deserved a tabernacle.

Some argue that the word for *tabernacle* simply means "tent or booth." It is important to notice that Peter does not propose to build six booths or tents, not even four (Jesus, Moses, Elijah, and the disciples). He is not simply proposing shelters. The Greek word used here is the same word used in the Greek translation of the Old Testament (Septuagint) for the tent of meeting during the Exodus, where God met with Israel (see Exodus 29:42). Perhaps, Peter thought that it would be a great idea to create three equal places where God could communicate with His people.

But God didn't think this was such a great idea. While Peter "was still speaking," God interrupts him. The imagery once again brings to memory the Exodus events. The cloud and the Voice were reminiscent of Moses' journey with the people of Israel. The Voice explains the interruption to Peter's proposition to make three shrines: " 'This is My beloved Son, with whom I am well-pleased; listen to Him!' " (Matthew 17:5).

There are three important clauses in God's message to them from the cloud. We will concentrate here on the last one: "Listen to Him!" God is actually quoting from Moses' own words that we discussed earlier: " 'The LORD your God will raise up for you a prophet like me . . . , you shall *listen to him*' " (Deuteronomy 18:15, emphasis added). Jesus did not come to destroy the Law and the

Prophets. He came to fulfill them.

God's revelation of Himself and His salvific plan through the Old Testament is important and not to be dismissed. It is Jesus' DNA. We know about Jesus through them. Nevertheless, God's revelation through Jesus, His beloved Son with whom He is well-pleased, supersedes all previous revelation. Not three tabernacles. Just one: the Son. Perhaps this very idea is what motivated Matthew's conclusion to this event. "And lifting up their eyes, they saw no one except Jesus Himself alone" (Matthew 17:8).

Matthew says that Jesus commanded the three disciples who were with Him not to share this vision until He had risen from the dead (verse 9). Perhaps only then would they understand His true identity as the glorified Son of God.

The greater Moses

Many other narratives in the Gospel of Matthew support this emphasis—Jesus is the new and greater Moses. Jesus reinterprets the Law in light of His mission. He fulfills the law. He is the true Moses who leads us out of slavery into the Promised Land. He guides us, teaches us, encourages us, and exhorts us as He leads us out of Egypt into the heavenly Canaan. May we listen to Him. May He be the one left standing in front of our eyes, until we see nothing else.

There is a hymn by Helen Lemmel that I have sung since my childhood. If you don't know the tune, add any tune you want and sing it with me, or just recite it.

Turn your eyes upon Jesus,
Look full in His wonderful face,
And the things of earth will grow strangely dim,
In the light of His glory and grace.

May this be our experience. Amen.

The Promise of His Rest

I am sure that by now you are wearing the "Matthean" glasses, that is, you are starting to read this Gospel through the eyes of Matthew's main proposals: Jesus is the Davidic Messiah King who was expected to come, Jesus is the new and greater Moses, Jesus fulfills the Old Testament prophecies and Jesus re-lives Israel's history becoming victorious where they failed. The portrayal of Jesus as the new Moses and the new Davidic Ruler permeates this Gospel and provides new "glasses" for us to more fully understand Matthew's message to his audience.

A few years ago, I decided to study a particular passage that appears only in this Gospel and that you have probably read before. It is found in Matthew 11:28–30, " 'Come to Me, all who are weary and heavy-laden, and I will give you rest. Take My yoke upon you and learn from Me, for I am gentle and humble in heart, and YOU WILL FIND REST FOR YOUR SOULS. For My yoke is easy and My burden is light.' "

I was particularly intrigued by the juxtaposition of this passage with the next two stories about the Sabbath (Matthew 12:1–14). I started wondering if this was a deliberate juxtaposition by Matthew being that Sabbath also means "rest" and therefore Jesus was proclaiming Himself the "provider of rest" (Matthew 11:28–30) and the " 'Lord of the Sabbath' " (12:1–8) in the same continuous narrative. This question became even more exciting as I realized that Matthew 12:1–14 contained the only two stories that occur on the Sabbath in the whole Gospel, which in itself fueled my curiosity because Matthew was writing to a predominantly Jewish audience and I would expect him to record more stories of Jesus that occurred on the Sabbath. I spent five years in this very passage, because this juxtaposition became the research for my dissertation (PhD in Biblical Studies).

The first few questions I had to ask were, What was the background of the word "rest" (*anapausis*) in the Greek Old Testament (Septuagint)? What was Jesus offering when He said "I will give you rest," and "you will find rest for your souls"? What did Matthew's audience understand when they heard such promises in light of their Greek translation of the Jewish Scriptures? Was this word (*anapausis*) related to Sabbath in any way?

Rest anyone?

I would like to share with you very briefly what I found. There are 137 occurrences of this root word in the Greek translation of the Old Testament. I went through each one of them. Of these occurrences, twenty-four are found in the Law (the Pentateuch), nineteen in the historical books, forty-four in the poetic books, and fifty in the prophetic books. In the Pentateuch, the main use of the term relates to a sabbatical rest to the Lord (whether on the seventh-day, the holy convocations of the seventh month, or on the seventh-year). Furthermore, sabbatical rest is the exclusive meaning of the term for Exodus and Leviticus, where the term is used only for this purpose.

In the historical and prophetic books, the prominent meaning given to this word is the promise of a "peaceful dwelling" for the people of God. This "rest" was promised to Israel through David and Solomon (see 2 Samuel 7:11; 1 Chronicles 22:9) and through the future Davidic Ruler (Jesus) that was to come (see Ezekiel 34:15, 23, 24). The Jewish people knew Sabbath as *anapausis,* and the Messianic age, which we call eternal life and/or heaven, as an age where every day would be Sabbath or *anapausis.* Their weekly Sabbath was a celebratory appetizer of heaven. Wow!

When Jesus offers all who are weary and burdened "rest for your souls," He is actually saying that those who heed His invitation now, enter the full meaning of the Sabbath rest, because they rest in Him, because Jesus is their Sabbath and this rest in Him was their weekly celebration. Furthermore, they would start experiencing the "age to come" now, in their souls, because Jesus is the one who offers and guarantees the eternal age of rest. I can't even start to tell you what incredible joy this understanding has brought into my own walk with Jesus Christ. He is *My rest*! He is *My sabbath*! I celebrate my redemption in Him every week!

There are so many things I would like to tell you, but it is difficult to summarize all the material in just a few words. There are very significant details in this passage, such as Matthew's use of *burden* in Matthew 11:30. Jesus said, "My burden is light." There is only one other place in all of Matthew's Gospel where the noun *burden* is used and it relates to the burden of Pharisaic legalism: " 'They tie up heavy *burdens* and lay them on men's shoulders' " (Matthew 23:4, emphasis added). Jesus' burden is light, the Pharisees' burden is heavy. This is the juxtaposition that Matthew is intending when, after Jesus' offer of rest, he records the story of the Pharisees observing that the disciples are not doing what is lawful to do on the Sabbath (Matthew 12:2). Jesus then challenges them to go back and read their Bibles! Jesus gives examples from the Law, the historic books, and the Prophets.

The True Rest

Jesus concludes His argument with a pronouncement: " 'The Son of Man is Lord of the Sabbath' " (Matthew 12:8). He sure is! The Sabbath finds its complete meaning in Him and His redemptive work! In chapter 12, Matthew manages to show that Jesus is greater than the temple (Matthew 12:6), greater than the prophets (Matthew 12:40), and greater than the greatest kings (Matthew 12:42). Jesus is greater than everything and everyone! And His yoke is easy and His burden is light!

Matthew follows this section with another story that occurs on the Sabbath (Matthew 12:9–14). Matthew then cites the longest Old Testament quotation found in his Gospel: Isaiah 42:1–4 (compare Matthew 12:18–21). This first of four songs recorded by Isaiah the prophet about God's Servant that was to come, specifically portrays Jesus' compassionate and graceful ministry:

> "A BATTERED REED He WILL NOT BREAK OFF,
> AND A SMOLDERING WICK He WILL NOT PUT OUT"
> (Matthew 12:20).

Have you ever felt like a battered reed, about to break? Have you ever felt like a smoldering wick, just smoke, no flame? I have. And during those times, Jesus' invitation to the "weary and heavy-laden" became personal and lifesaving. Would you join me in making this invitation personal? Read the following passage and place your name in the blank.

Jesus says to you: "Come to me, _____, weary and heavy-laden, and I will give you *rest*. Take My yoke upon you and learn from Me, for I am gentle and humble in heart, and *you will find rest for your soul*. For My Yoke is easy and My burden is light." I encourage you to accept His invitation. You will start experiencing heaven now, in your soul, because rest is not the absence of trouble, but the presence of Christ.

The Promise of His Forgiveness

My dear fellow traveler on the journey of life, have you ever felt like you have really betrayed God? I certainly have, and this segment of the Gospel of Matthew offers me assurance and peace. I am in awe of God's plan to forgive me. Just think about the cost! The cost of my forgiveness was the blood of Jesus! And now I live in the assurance that His blood is sufficient! He said, " 'This is My blood of the covenant, which is poured out for many for forgiveness of sins' " (Matthew 26:28). Wow, what a sacrifice! OK, I'm getting ahead of myself. If you want to follow the text closely, pause for a moment and read Matthew 26:14–27:10.

Betrayal introduced

In this segment of the Gospel, we discover that we are not alone in the betrayal of Jesus. His own disciples betrayed Him too. His disciples! Those who were the closest to Him and had spent years with Him! How could they? And then again, how could I?

Judas goes to the chief priests to negotiate a price on Jesus. The chief priests seemed to have been opposed to Jesus since the beginning of the Gospel (Matthew 2:4), and now they are ready to bargain! They've had it with Jesus. The price is set at thirty pieces of silver. At this time, you might want to get acquainted with a very interesting prophecy: Zechariah 11:12, 13. Matthew comes back to this prophecy further in the Gospel; later on we will return to it too.

The last Passover

Jesus and His disciples start talking about the Passover. The word *Passover* is repeated many times throughout these verses. They make plans (Matthew 26:17–19); the disciples follow Jesus' directions and prepare the Passover. The Passover was a memorial of redemption established when God delivered Israel out of slavery in Egypt. You can read about this symbolic meal in Exodus 12:21–24:

> Then Moses called for all the elders of Israel and said to them, "Go and take for yourselves lambs according to your families, and slay the Passover lamb. You shall take a bung of hyssop and dip it in the blood which is in the basin, and apply some of the blood that is in the basin to the lintel and the two doorposts; and none of you shall go outside the door of his house until morning. For the LORD will pass through to smite the Egyptians; and when He sees the blood on the lintel and on the two doorposts, the LORD will pass over the door and will not allow the destroyer to come in to your houses to smite you. And you shall observe this event as an ordinance for you and your children forever."

The blood on the doorposts would be a sign to the angel of death, and those inside the house would be safe from the last plague. What a powerful visualization of what the blood of Jesus was about to accomplish!

They begin the meal (Matthew 26:20). Jesus' first recorded words during this meal is an announcement that one of the disciples is about to betray Him. You mean, He knew about it and still ate with the betrayer? Wow! Then Jesus gives a sign to identify the traitor (verses 22–24). "And Judas, who was betraying Him, said, 'Surely it is not I, Rabbi?' Jesus said to him, 'You have said it yourself' " (verse 25). Read My lips! I know! And not just you, Judas, everyone is going to abandon Me tonight!

Oh, Jesus! My dear Jesus! You always seek to save, hoping we might relent from our rebellion. You never give up, forgiveness runs in Your veins, Your compassion and mercy surpass my comprehension!

The Lord's Supper

While Jesus and His disciples are having this meal, they are to recite the story of the Passover, called the *Haggadah.* This story narrates the details of that distant but eventful night. There are many symbols used as visual aids in this celebration—bread and cups are some of them.

While eating, Jesus takes some of the bread, and instead of saying the regular "this is the bread of affliction . . ." He modifies the Haggadah! He modifies it and applies it to Himself! I can imagine the disciples looking at Jesus, and thinking, *Jesus, did you forget the words?* They knew the words; they had celebrated the Passover for many, many years. Everyone knew the words, but Jesus knew the fulfillment of the words.

And so Matthew continues, "Jesus took some bread, and after a blessing, He broke it and gave it to the disciples, and said, 'Take, eat; this is My body' " (verse 26). Jesus, are You the Passover Lamb? (Paul answers affirmatively in 1 Corinthians 5:7.) Could it be that the ultimate fulfillment of the Passover points to our redemption, which is only possible through the blood of the Lamb of God?

He takes the cup, and again instead of reciting the regular text from the *Haggadah,* He explains its true fulfillment: "And when He had taken a cup and given thanks, He gave it to them, saying, 'Drink from it, all of you; for this is My blood of the covenant, which is poured out for many for forgiveness of sins.' " (verses 27, 28). His blood for all for forgiveness of sins. My heart leaps in joy and amazement!

The phrase "blood of the covenant" comes directly from Exodus 24:8. When God made a covenant with Israel through Moses, this covenant was ratified through blood. Jesus interprets and explains His death as a covenant sacrifice. His blood ratifies once and for all the covenant that God made to redeem the human race. And it covers all those who symbolically drink His blood in acceptance of His sacrifice for the forgiveness of their sins. These are the most significant and important good news for the human race recorded in the Scriptures—and anywhere for that matter.

But there is more.

This meal, which Jesus instituted by demonstrating that the bread and the cup were really symbols of His own death has been commonly called the eucharist. This word comes from the Greek verb *eucharisteō,* which means to give thanks. When Jesus took the cup, He gave thanks, and this is where the name for this Christian symbolic meal comes from. Jesus performed all four actions described in the preceding chapter: He took, He blessed or thanked, He broke, and He gave.

Having explained the reality of His broken body and poured out blood, Jesus makes a promise to His disciples: " 'But I say to you, I will not drink of this fruit of the vine from now on until that day when I drink it new with you in My Father's kingdom' " (Matthew 26:29). Once again, Jesus is talking about His everlasting kingdom, the Messianic age, the eternal life. I can't wait for that meal that we all will have together in heaven, celebrating the redemption achieved on the Cross! It is amazing that He promises this to those who are with Him. He says "when I drink it new with you," but the truth is that all of them would abandon Him that night. How could He make such a promise?

All fall away

Jesus is fully aware that all his disciples would stumble this night. They would flee and abandon him, yet He *still* makes promises to them. Amazing! If it weren't so, I wouldn't have a seat reserved in my name in the Messianic banquet—but I do! Praise be to Jesus Christ, my Savior and Lord!

"Then Jesus said to them, 'You will all fall away because of Me this night, for it is written, "I WILL STRIKE DOWN THE SHEPHERD AND THE SHEEP OF THE FLOCK WILL BE SCATTERED." But after I have been raised, I will go ahead of you to Galilee' " (verses 31, 32). What? Jesus knew and He still wanted to meet with them afterwards in Galilee? How can this be? What kind of God is this? The prophecy Jesus quotes comes from Zechariah 13:7. Once again Jesus is portrayed as the Shepherd King. In fulfillment of the prophecy, Jesus is the Shepherd who would be stricken, and His disciples are the sheep who would be scattered.

Peter, as always, is absolutely sure of himself. He tells Jesus that He is completely mistaken! Peter would stand alone, even if everyone else fall away (Matthew 26:33). I have been there also. I have felt as confident as Peter—only to fall so low that my big mouth was sealed shut forever, just like Peter's. Jesus compassionately says to Peter, " 'Truly I say to you that this very night, before a rooster crows, you will deny Me three times' " (verse 34). No way, insists Peter, " 'Even if I have to die with You, I will not deny You' " (verse 35). And all the disciples kept saying the same thing. I did too.

Peter and Judas

The juxtaposition of Peter and Judas has always caught my attention. Peter's denial and Judas's betrayal are narrated back to back, as if in one breath (Matthew 26:69–27:10). And yet, the end of each of their stories is *so* different: Peter would become a powerful preacher of the gospel within the newly formed Christian church; Judas would hang himself.

Peter's denial is narrated in detail in Matthew 26:69–75. Just as Jesus had predicted, Peter denied him three times. He denied Jesus with cursing and swearing, " 'I do not know the man!' " (Matthew 26:74). Then, after his vehement denial, "Peter remembered the word which Jesus had said, 'Before a rooster crows, you will deny Me three times.' And he went out and wept bitterly" (verse 75). *Wept bitterly!* That is a familiar scene for some of us.

Judas also starts to feel remorse when he realizes that Jesus had actually been condemned (Matthew 27:3). He comes to the chief priests and elders and says, " 'I have sinned by betraying innocent blood' " (verse 4). But they respond, "So what?" Judas desperately throws the silver on the floor and goes and hangs himself (verses 4, 5). What a tragic ending for such a skilled disciple! He could have done so much for the infant church! He had training, culture, skills, but he thought he had gone too far, that he had gone out of the reach of God's grace.

The chief priests, always careful to keep the law (even though they are about to kill God), start talking about the money on the floor. Because it is the price of blood (Jesus' blood! Worth much more, infinitely more than thirty pieces of silver!), they decide not to put it into the temple's treasury but buy the potter's field as a burial place for strangers (verses 6–8). In this way, a very interesting prophecy is fulfilled, which we discussed at the beginning of this chapter. Zechariah 11:12, 13 come to its ultimate fulfillment (see Matthew 27:9, 10). Read it! It's amazing.

Forgiveness for us

What made the difference between the two? What decides the ending of our story? I believe the key is found in Jesus' eucharistic words. If I come to believe that Jesus' blood is sufficient for the forgiveness of *my* sin, no matter how dark my betrayal and no matter how bitterly I have cried for it, I can find forgiveness. If you have betrayed Jesus terribly as I have, then I invite you to believe. Believe that Jesus meant what He said that day. Believe that His grace is sufficient. And when you come to accept His truth, you will live with the assurance and the joyful expectation that you will drink with Jesus anew in the coming kingdom, because His blood has purchased a ticket for you to get there!

Now, let's do an *incarnational* reading of Jesus' eucharistic words. Every time there is a blank space, place your name in it.

Let's say it aloud so that we never forget it! "Drink from it,
_____; for this is My blood of the covenant, which
is poured out for _____ for forgiveness of
_____'s sins. But I say to you, _____, I will not
drink of this fruit of the vine from now on until that day when I
drink it new with you, _____, in My Father's kingdom."

Woohoo! Don't be surprised now, if you get an irresistible urge
to start preaching and teaching the gospel of the good news of Jesus Christ! That's what happened to Peter and me—and I can't
stop!

The Promise of His Redemption

We are approaching the end of our journey together. There is so much more to be said and analyzed. The Bible is like a deep well—we never cease to find new and refreshing perspectives about our beloved Jesus. We now arrive at a very solemn and amazing section of the Gospel: Jesus' crucifixion. For a Jew, a crucified Messiah would be an oxymoron. *Messiah* means "Anointed One" in Hebrew (*Christ* means "Anointed One" in Greek). The Messiah would be God's Servant, a victorious Ruler. How could He be crucified? No, these two words could not co-exist! Or could they?

Imagine yourself as a first century Jew. You have been expecting the coming of a Davidic ruler who would take control and establish his kingdom. Then Jesus comes, He seems to be the One! Then He dies. How could a Jewish follower of Jesus come to understand that His death was an atoning sacrifice for sin? There are three main obstacles in the Jewish mind that would complicate matters:

1. Human sacrifices were not allowed by the God of Israel, as they were pagan practices (Deuteronomy 12:31).
2. One person was not allowed to die in place of another (Deuteronomy 24:16).
3. Death by crucifixion was considered a curse (Deuteronomy 21:22, 23).

Somehow, Jesus would have to interpret His death in a way that they could understand. The Gospels propose that Jesus interpreted His death in light of the Jewish Scriptures by using phrases and terms that would explain His death as a salvific sacrifice. (Before I go on, I want to reiterate my indebtedness to my mentor and professor, Dr. Lynn Losie. Most of the material posted in this paragraph and the next come directly from his notes and are used with his permission.)

Jesus' death as atoning sacrifice

These are the four most prominent ways in which Jesus interpreted His death in light of the Jewish Scriptures in the book of Matthew:

1. Jesus interpreted His death as the *vicarious suffering of the Servant of Yahweh.* To understand this explanation, compare Matthew 20:28 with Isaiah 53.
2. Jesus interpreted His death as a *covenant sacrifice.* To understand Jesus' interpretation, read Matthew 26:27, 28 in light of the events recorded in Exodus 24:3–8.
3. Jesus interpreted His death as the *sacrifice of the beloved Son.* For more information read Matthew 21:33–45 and Mark 12: 1-2 with the Old Testament story of the beloved son recorded in Genesis 22.
4. Jesus interpreted His death as the *suffering of the Righteous One.* This last interpretation of Jesus' death is the focus of this chapter. We will compare Matthew 27:33–54 and Psalm 22. It would be a good idea to read these passages now, before you continue reading.

Forsaken

Matthew narrates Jesus' crucifixion using words and terms from Psalm 22. For example, consider Matthew 27:35, "And when they crucified Him, they divided up His garments among themselves by casting lots." And now, compare that with Psalm 22:18, "They divide my garments among them, / And for my clothing they cast lots." Let's read a few more verses from Matthew: "And those passing by were hurling abuse at Him, wagging their heads. . . . 'HE TRUSTS IN GOD; LET GOD RESCUE HIM NOW, IF HE DELIGHTS IN HIM; for He said, "I am the Son of God" ' " (Matthew 27:39, 43). Back to Psalm 22,

> All who see me sneer at me;
> They separate with the lip, they wag the head, saying,
> "Commit yourself to the LORD; let Him deliver him;
> Let Him rescue him, because He delights in him" (verses 7, 8).

One more: Psalm 22:16,

> For dogs have surrounded me; A band of evildoers has encompassed me; They pierced my hands and my feet.

Can you believe that this Psalm was written one thousand years before Jesus' death? How amazing that God would inspire David with such prophetic words! Prophecies fill me with awe! I serve a God who is sovereign.

Psalm 22 is the Psalm of the Righteous Sufferer. The cry of anguish comes from one who has been faithful to God (verses 8–10). Jesus cried out: " 'MY GOD, MY GOD, WHY HAVE YOU FORSAKEN ME?' " (Matthew 27:46), quoting Psalm 22:1. Jesus understood His death as that of a sinless Victim, a righteous Sufferer. Matthew points out that this occurred about the ninth hour (3 P.M.). This time would place Jesus' death at the time of the slaughter of the Passover lamb. No wonder other New Testament writers make a direct connection between Jesus and the Passover lamb! (See 1 Corinthians 5:7, "Christ our Passover also has been sacrificed.")

Death victory?

Matthew's narrative of Jesus' death is the most dramatic of all four Gospels. He mentions that the veil of the temple was torn in two, from top to bottom; and he also mentions that there was an earthquake, the earth shook and the rocks split (Matthew 27:51). Matthew can't wait to tell us that Jesus' death on the cross is, in fact, a victory! He can't wait until Sunday morning. So after letting us know that there was an earthquake, he records the following event: "The tombs were opened, and many bodies of the saints who had fallen asleep were raised; and coming out of the tombs after His resurrection they entered the holy city and appeared to many" (verses 52, 53). Wow! A corporate resurrection! In the moment Jesus dies! What happened?

Well, there was a long awaited expectation that when the Messianic age started, when the Davidic King would start his everlasting reign, the dead would rise to life (see Isaiah 26:19; Daniel 12:2). Matthew is announcing that through Jesus' death this new age has started. Full victory has been gained over death! And it's not even Sunday morning yet. Matthew's view of the Cross as a victory is consistent with the rest of the Gospel. Jesus is King! He is in control! He is the ultimate Victor!

He lives!

I absolutely love the language Matthew uses for Resurrection morning. Another earthquake: "For an angel of the Lord descended from heaven and came and rolled away the stone and sat upon it" (Matthew 28:2). Sat on it! This is so like Matthew! Sitting on the throne type of language, except that this time the angel *sat* on the stone of Jesus' tomb. Death has been conquered! Think about it for a moment. Imagine the angel sitting on the stone that was placed in front of Jesus' tomb. The angel sat on it—*sat on it!* I love it! Way to go, Matthew!

Jesus met with His disciples and they worshiped Him. Oh, I

THE PROMISE OF HIS REDEMPTION

would have loved to have been there, seeing and worshiping the resurrected Christ!

At the end of the Gospel, Matthew summarizes several topics that he has developed: Jesus' full authority, His commission to go to all nations, His role as the new and greater Moses, and His reminder that He is with us always until the end of the world. He is truly Immanuel. "And Jesus came up and spoke to them, saying, 'All authority has been given to Me in heaven and on earth. Go therefore and make disciples of all the nations, baptizing them, in the name of the Father and the Son and the Holy Spirit, teaching them to observe all that I commanded you; and lo, I am with you always, even to the end of the age' " (Matthew 28:18–20).

I am not sure where you were when we started this journey together. Perhaps you were in a tomb, a cave, or a valley, but I know one thing: Matthew has a superencouraging message for you! Throughout the pages of his Gospel, he reminds us that Jesus is the Davidic King and His throne is forever.

He also tells us that Jesus lived a perfect life on our behalf. He is the new and greater Moses, who guides us into the Promised Land as He fulfills all Jewish Messianic expectations. He has been true to the prophecies and promises of His protection, blessing, presence, guidance, perfection, provision, supremacy, rest, forgiveness, and redemption. All authority has been given to Jesus in heaven and on earth! The Gospel ends with Jesus' victory speech. Elections are over! The balloons are falling! And He is soon coming back to take over the world forever—and take us home!

In those cloudy and foggy days when you are feeling blue, when you can't see anything because the fog is thick, remember *the angel sat on the stone!*

May you be blessed with the MEGAJOY of your salvation in Jesus Christ!